LES NOCES

LES NOCES
in Full Score

Igor Stravinsky

DOVER PUBLICATIONS
Garden City, New York

Bibliographical Note

This Dover edition, first published in 1998, is an unabridged republication of the work originally published by J. & W. Chester, Ltd., London, 1922. It incorporates new lists of contents and instrumentation; a glossary and preface; and "A Note on the Translation" and "Translation of the French Text" by Stanley Appelbaum, both prepared specially for this edition. The Preface has been adapted from Chapter III of Eric Walter White's *Stravinsky: A Critical Survey, 1882–1946* (Dover, 1997). The illustrations on pages xii and xxiv (both from the collection of Lord Berners) are reproduced from the same source.

International Standard Book Number

ISBN-13: 978-0-486-40413-4
ISBN-10: 0-486-40413-7

Manufactured in the United States by LSC Communications Book LLC
40413707   2021
www.doverpublications.com

CONTENTS

LES NOCES
The Wedding

Russian Choreographic Scenes
in Four Tableaux, with Song and Music

For Solo Vocal Quartet (SM-sTB)
Chorus (SATB), Four Pianos and Percussion

(Composed 1914–17)

PART ONE

PART TWO

INSTRUMENTATION

Solo Vocal Quartet (SM-sTB)
Chorus (SATB)

4 Pianos

Percussion
    Side Drum with snare [Caisse claire à timbre, C.cl.à.t.]
    Side Drum without snare [Caisse claire sans timbre, C.cl.s.t.]
    Field Drum with snare [Tambour à timbre, Tmb.à.t.]
    Field Drum without snare [Tambour sans timbre, Tmb.s.t.]
    Bass Drum [Grosse Caisse, Gr.C., G.C.]
    Timpani [Timpani, Timp.]

    Cymbals [Piatti]
    Tambourine [Tambour de Basque, T.d.B.]
    Triangle [Triang(olo), Tr.]
    Xylophone [Xyloph(one), Xyl.]

    Two Crotales* [Crotales]
    Bell* [Cloche]

    [Playing instructions for percussion are translated in the glossary, p. xi.]

*The two crotales are played by the musician who plays the snareless drums. The bell is played by the xylophonist. Pitches for the crotales and bell first appear on p. 127.
On p. 132, twelve measures from the end, the pitch D-sharp for the lower crotale (instead of its reiterated, established C-sharp) appears to be an error; there is no corresponding doubling in the pianos.

GLOSSARY OF FRENCH PLAYING INSTRUCTIONS

arraché, ripped ["snapped off" piano arpeggios]
assez fort, rather loud
avec, with
    deux mains, with two hands
    le genou, with [strike on] the knee
    le pouce, with the thumb [tambourine "thumb roll"]

bag(uette[s]), beater(s), stick(s) [but misspelled "bagh.," p. 67]
    de Triangle, triangle beater (thin metal rod)
    en bois, wood beater
    en métal, metal beater
    molle(s), soft-tipped beater(s)
bois, wood [beater]

en dehors, from a distance
et, and
étouffez, damp
et toujours, and always
excessivement fort, excessively loud

fausset, falsetto
fort, très martelé, strong, very articulated ["hammered out"]
"fr⁓" signifie frôler la membrane avec le pouce, [this sign] indicates
    a "thumb roll" [footnote, p. 24]
frôler, rub [the tambourine head]

genou, [strike on the] knee

jouées par les musiciens du Xyl. et des C.cl. et Tmb.s.t., played by the
    musicians [who play] the xylophone and the snareless drums
    [see footnote, p. ix]

lâchez, bring out ["let loose"]

m.dr. [main droite], right hand
m.g. [main gauche], left hand

ordinairement, [play] in the usual way

partie du Tmb. de B., tambourine part
péd. gauche, left ["soft" or "una corda"] pedal of the piano
pouce, thumb
préparez, prepare [to play]
    les Crotales, prepare the crotales
    le Si♭, prepare the B-flat [timpani tuning]
    le sol aigu, prepare the upper G [timpani tuning]

reprenez le Tmb. de B., take up the tambourine once again
roul. [roulement, roulade], [drum] roll

sons réels, actual pitches

très, very
    bref et sec, very short and detached ["dry"]
    court, very short
    fort et détaché, very loud and detached
    rythmé (et très court) et bien martelé, very rhythmic
       (and very short) and strongly articulated ["hammered"]
    sec, very detached ["dry"]
    sonore, very sonorous, resonant

(le) Xylophone prépare la Cloche, the xylophone [player] prepares
    [to play] the bell

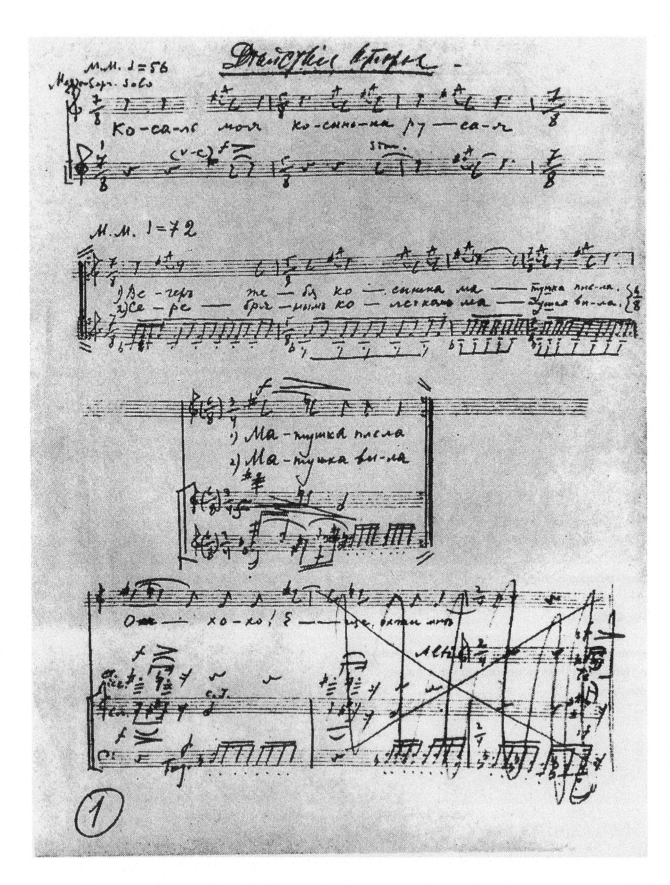

Early MS. sketch (*ca.* 1915) of the opening of *Les Noces*, Tableau I.
(*From the collection of Lord Berners*)

PREFACE

[DURING STRAVINSKY'S return from Italy, in 1917, to Morges, Switzerland,] considerable progress had been made with the last part of *The Wedding*. Stravinsky had turned one of the attic rooms at the Villa Mornand (to which he had recently moved from the Villa Rogivue) into a studio, which was reached by a half-hidden wooden staircase well barricaded by doors; and there he could work undisturbed on the vocal and piano score. Ramuz,[1] who had again been enlisted to make the French translation of the Russian text, has described how of a summer afternoon the sound of the composer at his piano (and his percussion instruments, whenever a hand was disengaged!) could be heard in the little square outside, where two or three women were usually to be found sitting on a bench and knitting in the shade of the trees, and how they would raise their heads for a moment in bewilderment and then, with an indulgent '*C'est le monsieur russe!*' resume their knitting. The work was finished by the end of the year; but as it had been promised to Diaghilev[2] and there appeared to be no possibility of its being produced until after the war, the question of its instrumentation was for the moment shelved.

Although in the published score the work is subtitled 'Russian Choreographic Scenes,' it is really a cantata for choir, four soloists . . . and accompanying orchestra in four tableaux played through without interruption. . . . There is no plot in the usual sense—in fact, Stravinsky's intention was that it should be staged as a kind of *divertissement*, a scenic ceremony in which he would make absolutely free use of both pagan and Christian elements in Russian village wedding ritual and customs—but the score carries sufficient indications to give an outline of the action. . . .

The most remarkable thing about *The Wedding* is that, despite its long period of gestation—it took Stravinsky three and a half years to compose and another five before the instrumentation was completed—it is of all his works the one that makes the greatest impression of unity. The original conception was his own; it was he who compiled and adapted the text from Kirieievsky's Collection of Popular Poems; the melodic material nearly all springs from a single cell by a process of 'budding'; and, with two brief exceptions, the whole work is geared to metronome rates of 80 and 120 to the minute. Cocteau has compared *The Wedding* to a racing car: but it is not so much its speed that impresses as the smooth and regular running of its well-oiled engine.

This extraordinary unity of conception and execution is obtained only at the expense of a certain monotony, for there is no great variety or contrast in the musical materials employed. The first part consists of song alternating with lamentation; the second part, of song alternating with a comic element. As Victor Belaiev explains in his excellent study of *The Wedding*, 'the lamentation shows itself to be the static element—during it the modulational movement of the music is suspended, and there remains only the steadfast harmonic background on which the voice embroiders its melodic pattern'—whereas the comic element 'is distinguished by strongly marked musical characteristics, based on the clever use of syncopated rhythms and the sudden addition of choral voices to the solo voice.'. . .

All this melodic material is original, with the following exceptions: The bridegroom's request for a blessing[3] is taken from a collection of liturgical chants for the Octave services. A popular Russian factory song, which had been noted down by Stravinsky's friend Mitusov, plays an important part in the scene of the wedding feast.[4] And one of the themes in the same scene[5] is a reminiscence of the drunken singing of two Vaudois revellers who were with Stravinsky in the funicular when he was returning from Château d'Oex to Clarens one day at the end of January 1915. This incoherent theme, syncopated by hiccups, consists of an alternation of 4/4 and 3/4 bars. It is typical of Stravinsky's method that its melody should be changed to fit the fundamental motif, while its characteristic rhythm is retained; and, so transformed, it becomes the main subject of the last part of the final tableau.[6] In fact, it is used to bring the work to an end;[7] and there its slow, deliberate deployment (in 3/4 time) is punctuated by the tolling of the bell chord, which is so spread out that, with the exception of an extra bar's rest of three beats just before section 135, it occurs on every eighth beat. As the voices cease singing, pools of silence come flooding in between the measured strokes of the bell chord, and the music dies away in a miraculously fresh and radiant close.

Although the composition of *The Wedding* was finished by the beginning of 1918, it took Stravinsky another five years to find the right orchestral formula. According to Schaeffner,[8] his original idea had been 'to establish two categories of sound: *wind* (including voices) and *percussion*: the first would be provided by the choir, woodwind and brass, the second by two string orchestras, the one playing pizzicato and the other with the bow. Only a few pages were written of a score needing about 150 players for performance, which made the work practically unplayable.' At this point Stravinsky thought of a simpler solution, consisting of an electrically driven pianola and harmonium, a group of percussion instruments and two cymbaloms of different compass; but although the first two tableaux were instrumented on these lines, the difficulties of synchronisation proved too great, and this project too was abandoned. When, after the war, Diaghilev ultimately decided to produce the cantata as a ballet, Stravinsky was forced to find a definitive solution, and in 1921 he made up his mind merely to accompany the voices with an orchestra of percussion divided into instruments with and without definite pitch: four (non-mechanical) pianos, xylophone, timpani, two crotales and a bell, as opposed to two side drums (with and without snare), two drums (with and without snare), tambourine, bass drum, cymbals and triangle. . . . [W]hether it

---

[1] [Charles-Ferdinand Ramuz. For other commentary on Stravinsky's collaboration with this Swiss author, see the opening of A Note on the Translation in this edition.]

[2] [Serge Diaghilev, the Russian impresario.]

[3] Section 50.

[4] Sections 110, 120, 124, 125, 130–2.

[5] Sections 91, 127 and 129.

[6] It appears in the vocal parts at sections 114, 121 and 122, and in the orchestra at sections 93, 115, 116 and 126.

[7] Cf. the bass solo at section 133 and the orchestral coda beginning six bars before section 135.

[8] [Biographer André Schaeffner.]

was Stravinsky's intention or not, the peculiar timbre of the orchestra in *The Wedding* definitely recalls one of those mechanical pianos with drum-, cymbal- and bell-attachment that are to be found in out-of-the-way inns in Madrid, Russia or the Alps and, when the mechanism has been set in motion by a coin, break with a whirr like a startled pheasant into a clatter of gay noise to cheer the festive guests.

The Wedding was ultimately produced by the Russian Ballet on June 13, 1923, at the Théâtre de la Gaîté, Paris, with choreography by Bronislava Nijinska. When three years later Diaghilev brought it to the His Majesty's Theatre, London, with Georges Auric, Francis Poulenc, Vittorio Rieti and Vladimir Dukelsky as the four pianists, there was an outburst of dismay from the critics that equalled in intensity their reaction to *The Rite of Spring* thirteen years earlier. The virulence of this attack so exasperated H. G. Wells that on June 18, 1926, he wrote an open letter, which was printed and distributed as a hand-out with the ballet programme. In it he said: 'Writing as an old-fashioned popular writer, not at all of the highbrow sect, I feel bound to bear my witness on the other side. I do not know of any other ballet so interesting, so amusing, so fresh or nearly so exciting as *Les Noces*. I want to see it again and again, and because I want to do so I protest again this conspiracy of wilful stupidity that may succeed in driving it out of the programme. . . . That ballet is a rendering in sound and vision of the peasant soul, in its gravity, in its deliberate and simpleminded intricacy, in its subtly varied rhythms in its deep undercurrents of excitement, that will astonish and delight every intelligent man or woman who goes to see it. The silly pretty-pretty tradition of Watteau and Fragonard is flung aside. Instead of fancy dress peasants we have peasants in plain black and white, and the smirking flirtatiousness of Daphnis and Chloe gives place to a richly humorous solemnity. It was an amazing experience to come out from this delightful display with the warp and woof of music and vision still running and interweaving in one's mind, and find a little group of critics flushed with resentment and ransacking the stores of their minds for cheap trite depreciation of the freshest and strongest thing that they had had a chance to praise for a long time.'

From Eric Walter White's
Stravinsky: A Critical Survey, 1882–1946[9]

[9]Dover, 1997 (0-486-29755-1).

A NOTE ON THE TRANSLATION

ALTHOUGH STRAVINSKY made it clear that the Russian text of *Les Noces* (*Svádebka*) was the primary one—the one that suggested the music to him, the one he preferred to have sung—it is a text that offers special difficulties to a translator. Based on rustic folksongs and special regional traditions, it bristles with rarefied vocabulary and word forms. For those interested in further study, or performance, of the Russian text, a useful transliteration, by Marc Gwynne (in libretto form; that is, without the incessant incantatory word repetitions, and not indicating the distribution of the text among the vocal parts), is to be found in the booklet to the 1991 compact disc Hyperion CDA66410, *Stravinsky: Les Noces and Other Choral Music.* The same booklet includes an English text ("reprinted by kind permission of J G W Chester/Edition Wilhelm Hansen London Ltd"), also in libretto form, that is definitely based on the Russian text but is far from being strictly literal.

The French text, though decidedly not a straight translation of the Russian,* is not to be scorned. It was adapted from the Russian, under the composer's supervision, by the French-Swiss novelist Ramuz, who also adapted *Renard* and wrote the original text of *Histoire du Soldat.* Moreover, Ramuz' French version, which has been termed "masterly," is frequently performed and recorded. Therefore, it seemed sensible (as well as perfectly feasible) to take the French text as the basis for the present absolutely literal and absolutely complete translation, including each and every word repeat. To add to its usefulness, the translation is keyed to the printed rehearsal numbers and indicates exactly which voices are involved at each point; passages sung simultaneously to different sets of words are indicated by long brackets in the margin. All phrases in parentheses, either giving stage directions or identifying the voices with particular members of the wedding, are strictly translations of items in the printed score; none of them has been added by the translator. An occasional explanation by the translator appears within square brackets.

STANLEY APPELBAUM

---

*The French text always conveys the same sentiments, the same moods and the same "plot elements" as the Russian, but often differs substantially in details. To take only three typical examples chosen at random: (1) The Russian text corresponding to rehearsal numbers [12] and [13] translates as: "Sir Khvetis Pamfilevich, you have a nightingale in your garden, in the lofty tower chamber, in the lofty room that is thoroughly decorated, in the daytime he whistles and all night long he sings." (2) The Russian text sung by the chorus at number [87] translates as: "A berry rolled downhill with another berry; the berry bowed in greeting to the other berry." (3) In [123] the Russian words of the Bass soloist translate as: "Along the street, street, yea, along the wide street the young man walked, strolled; his head was covered with a furry hat."

TRANSLATION OF THE FRENCH TEXT

Participants in order of appearance

S^s = solo soprano (sometimes portraying "The Bride")

S.A. = chorus sopranos and altos (sometimes portraying "The Bride's Female Friends")

M^s or M.S^s = solo mezzo-soprano

T^s = solo tenor (sometimes portraying "The [Groom's] Father" and "A Male Guest")

B^s = solo bass (sometimes portraying "The Groom," "The Best Man," "The Groom's Father" and "The Male Matchmaker")

T.B. = chorus tenors and basses (there are also solos for one basso profondo from the chorus)

The bracketed numbers in the script refer to the circled rehearsal numbers in the score.

(In [36] ff., all the soloists represent "The [Groom's] Parents, in turn"; in [98] ff., they are "The Best Man, the Groom's Mother, the Male Matchmaker and the Female Matchmaker, in turn"; in [110], T^s and B^s, together, are "A Male Guest on the Bride's Side"; see score and translation for further group characterizations as "Girls," "Guests," "Everybody," etc.)

To Serge Diaghilev

THE WEDDING

PART ONE
Scene One: The Braid

[The bride is named Anastasia Timofeyevna; the groom is named Khvetis (in the French: Fétis) Pamfilevich]

S^s: Braid, braid, my braid, my braid! [1] My mother braided you carefully in the evening—

S.A.: She braided you!

S^s: Braid, she combed you with a silver comb—

S.A.: She combed you!

S^s (*The Bride*): Woe, woe is me, woe once again!

[2] S.A. (*The Bride's Female Friends*): Nastasia's hair is being braided, it will be braided; Timofeyevna's hair will be braided; the braid will be combed, then it will be braided—

M^s: With a beautiful red ribbon.

[3] S.A.: Nastasia's hair is being braided, it will be braided; Timofeyevna's hair will be braided; you will be braided, you will be well combed, O braid, with the fine comb.

[4] S^s (*The Bride*): One day, who came? It was the female matchmaker, the spiteful one, the envious one, the heartless one, the merciless one. [5] She started to pinch the girl, to pull her braid—

S.A.: To pull her braid . . .

[6] S^s: To pull the braid, to pinch the girl, then to part the braid—

S.A.: To part it . . .

S^s: Woe, woe is me, woe once again!

[7] S.A. (*The Bride's Female Friends*): Nastasia's hair is being braided, it will be braided; Timofeyevna's hair will be braided; the braid will be combed, then it will be braided—

M.S^s: With a beautiful red ribbon—

[8] M.S^s, S.A.: With a beautiful blue ribbon.

S^s (*The Bride*): My braid, my beautiful braid.

[9] S.A.: Console yourself, console yourself, little bird; don't cry, my dear Nastasia; don't be upset; don't cry, don't cry, my darling Timofeyevna.

[10] T^s: Even though you are going away—

T^s, B^s: You are going away over yonder—

S.A.: A nightingale sings there for you.

[11] B^s: Your father-in-law will open his arms wide for you when you come—

S[s], B[s]: And your mother-in-law will greet you with respect, with kindness, with tenderness, and will love you.

[12] S[s], M[s], S.A.: Sir Khvetis Pamfilevich, a beautiful tree is in your garden, in the tree a nightingale sings; [13] isn't he singing to make her happy?—singing night and day, singing to her up there about his love.

[14] S[s], M[s], T[s], B[s], S.A.: It's for you, Nastasia Timofeyevna, it's for you that he sings and will sing, [15] he will sing his most beautiful song for you, he'll let you sleep, he'll wake you up for Mass.

[16] S[s], M[s], T[s], B[s], S.A.T.B.: Go, go! Sing, little bird, sing; sing, bird on your bough; [17] go, go! Nastasia will be pleased; start and start over again; go!

B[s]: And may all things be Sunday for her.

[18] B[s], B: In the moss a brook flows . . .

S[s], M[s], B[s]: In the moss a brook flows; they came there, they sat down there. [19] They laugh, they drink, the drum beats . . . They laugh, they drink, the drum beats. The flute plays, all the women spin around and all the men shove one another.

[20] S.A.: Our well-beloved Nastasia is brought for her wedding, brought to us.

[21] (*The Bride and Her Mother*):

S[s]: Braid my hair for me properly; [22] it should be tight on top, [23] less so in the middle, and at the tip a beautiful blue ribbon.

T[s], B[s]: Most lovable mother, be so good, be so good as to enter our cottage to help the female matchmaker, [22] be so good, be so good as to help the female matchmaker undo the braid, unknot the braid [23] of blonde Nastasia, of blonde Nastasia, who is to be married.

[24] S.A. (*The Bride's Female Friends*): Nastasia's hair is being braided, it will be braided; Timofeyevna's hair will be braided. It will be braided [25] once again, and from bottom to top and from top to bottom her hair will be combed, then her hair will be braided with a beautiful red ribbon. [26] Nastasia's hair is being braided, it will be braided; Timofeyevna's hair will be braided; the braid will be combed; it will be well combed with the fine comb.

[25] S[s]: A beautiful blue ribbon, a beautiful red ribbon, a ribbon red as my cheeks, [26] a blue ribbon, blue as my eyes.

Scene Two: In the Groom's House

[27] T[s], B[s], A.T.B.: Be so good, lovable mother, be so good as to enter the cottage, be so good as to help us undo the groom's curls; [28] be so good as to untangle the curly-haired man's curls. Mother, come into the cottage; be so good as to help us undo the curls.

[29] T[s]: With what shall we comb Khvetis' curls?

B[s]: With what shall we make Pamfilevich's curls shine?

[30] T.B.: Be so good as to enter the cottage; lovable mother, be so good as to help the female matchmaker undo the curls.

[31] B[s]: Quickly, friends, let us rush to the city's three markets; [32] with what shall we make the curly-haired man's curls shine?

T[s]: And there, there we shall find a bottle [32] of oil with which to make the groom's curls shine.

[33] T.B.: Lovable mother, be so good, be so good as to enter our cottage, be so good as to help us undo the curls.

[34] T[s]: To undo the curls, to untangle the curls.

[35] M[s]: Last night, last night Khvetis was still at home.

T[s] (*The [Groom's] Father*): He was combing his blonde hair, he was showing how handsome he is.

[36–39] (*The [Groom's] Parents, in turn*):

M[s]: And whose are you now, beautiful blonde curls? And whose are you now, beautiful round curls? Whose are the curls? Whose is the boy? So, you see, Nastasia, tend to them. . . . Oh, the handsome curly-haired man! . . . His poor mother who curled his hair, while she was curling it, lamented:

B[s]: They belong to the red-cheeked girl with a name like Nastasia Timofeyevna. . . . Oh, curls of the curly-haired man, let's see how you curl, let's see how you wave, oh, waves of the wavy-haired man!

S[s]: The curls of the curly-haired man, and she curls him, also she tends the curly-haired man; oh, curls of the curly-haired man, let's see how you curl, let's see how you wave, oh, waves of the wavy-haired man!

T[s]: The comb is dipped in raspberry kvass . . . while curling, she lamented:

[40] S.A.: "My son, my dear son, whom I carried for nine months—

T[s]: Dear child to whom I gave birth—

S.A.: Now another woman will have you—

T[s]: And another woman will love you—

B[s]: And another woman will curl your hair!"

[41] S[s]: Whose are the beautiful blonde curls, the well-untangled ones, the nice and round ones, the so well-oiled ones, the so well-tended ones, the so well-curl-papered ones, the so well-arranged ones!

[42] & [43] B[s]: Glory, honor to the parents; the father and the mother have made a fine child. . . . Everywhere, everywhere, everywhere, even in Moscow, all the girls throw their arms around his neck.

M[s]: They made him sweet, well-behaved and prudent, proud, reasonable and obedient. . . . Everywhere, everywhere, even in Moscow, all the girls throw their arms around his neck.

S[s]: Fall into place, blonde curls, all around and in front. And you, Nastasia, grow accustomed to the strapping young fellow he is, even if it doesn't suit you.

T[s]: And you, Nastasiushka, grow accustomed to the strapping young fellow he is, the strapping young fellow he is, even if it doesn't suit you.

B.: Everywhere, everywhere, even in Moscow, all the girls throw their arms around his neck.

S.A.T.: To the strapping young fellow he is, even if it doesn't suit you.

[44] & [45] A.T.B.: Be so good, lovable mother, be so good as to enter our cottage, be so good as to help us undo the groom's curls, be so good as to untangle the curly-haired man's curls. Mother, enter our cottage, be so good as to help us undo the curls.

T[s], B[s]: The groom's curls, the curly-haired man's curls.

[46] S[s], M[s], T[s], S.A.T.: Holy Mother, be kind; Holy Mother, come in person—

B.: Come with us, come with us—

[47] Sˢ, Mˢ, Tˢ, S.A.T.: Most Holy Mother of Jesus Christ—

B.: Come with us, come with us—

[48] Sˢ, Mˢ, Tˢ, S.A.T.: And the Apostles, the angels also—

B.: Come with us, come with us—

[49] Sˢ, Mˢ, Tˢ, S.A.T.: May God bless us, may God bless us, and His Son; come with us, come with us, come with us.

[50–52] Bˢ & a basso-profondo chorus member (*The Groom*): And you, father and mother, bless your child, who approaches proudly, knocking down every wall in order to seize his intended, to enter the church and kiss the silver cross.

Sˢ, Mˢ, S.A.: There, where Sir Khvetis is, there also the candles, the candles burn, and there Our Lady awaits him.

[53] & [54] Bˢ (*The Best Man*): Vagabonds, hoboes and all you good-for-nothings, brothers, come, so that he can set out happily and take what is destined to him.

Sˢ, Mˢ, S.A.: Everyone bless the young prince who is about to wed . . . so that he can take his stand beneath the golden crown.

[55] Sˢ, Mˢ, Tˢ, Bˢ, S.A.T.B. (*Everybody*): Ho!

T.B.: As the feather falls and the flower bends—

Sˢ, Mˢ, Tˢ, Bˢ, S.A.T.B.: The flower bends—

T.B.: The flower bends, the feather falls—

[56] Sˢ, Mˢ, Tˢ, Bˢ, S.T.B.: The feather falls—

T.B.: Thus, before his father, he has let himself fall—

Sˢ, Mˢ, S.A: Thus, before his mother, he has bent his knees—

T.B.: He has said: [57] Bless you child so he may depart beneath the eye of God—

Sˢ, Mˢ, S.A.: Depart, under His protection— . . . set out after them.

T.B.: And the saints' also, so he may set out after them.

[58] Tˢ: Lord God, bless us all, from the greatest to the smallest; Lord, bless all of us, us members of the wedding, ho!

Bˢ: Lord God, bless us all . . . ho!

Sˢ, Mˢ, S.: May Saint Damian bless us, too . . . as you did for our parents, ho!

A.: . . . as you did for our parents, ho!

T.B.: . . . ho!

[59] T.B.: May God bless us and the whole family, may God bless us and the son and the daughter, may God bless us and the father and the mother—

Tˢ, Bˢ: . . . the whole family . . . the son and the daughter . . . the father and the mother . . .

Sˢ, Mˢ, S.A.: . . . the mother and the father . . .

[60] T.B.: May God bless us and the sister and the brother, may God bless us and all those who fear Him and are faithful to Him—

Sˢ, Mˢ, Tˢ, Bˢ, S.A.: . . . the sister and the brother . . . all those who fear Him and are faithful to Him—

[61] Sˢ, Mˢ, Tˢ, Bˢ, S.A.T.B.: May God keep us and assist us, may God bless us! Come with us! Come with us! Come with us!

[62] T.B.: Come with us! Saint Luke as well, Saint Luke, Saint Luke!

S.A.: Come with us, Saint Luke as well—

[63] & [64] T.B.: Watch over those who are setting up a household.

S.A.: Preside over their household.

T.B.: Arrange everything, Saint Luke, in the best way for them, both of them chosen, promised one to the other; protect them, protect them at all times, them and their children!

S.A.: . . . chosen by you yourself, assist them, protect them, protect them, them and their children!

Sˢ, Mˢ, Tˢ: . . . Assist them in the present and at all times, them and their children!

Bˢ: . . . them and their children!

Scene Three: The Departure of the Bride

[65] & [66] S.A.: Just as one sees in the sky the white moon and the sun, thus the princess lived in the palace, lived with her old father, and she was happy beside her father and mother.

[67] Tˢ: Bless me, father, I am leaving—

Sˢ, Mˢ, S.A.: And I shall never come back again.

[68] (*The Father and the Mother*):

Bˢ: Just see! Just as the beautiful yellow candle melts in front of the icon and then sticks to the foot—

Sˢ: . . . thus the swift feet found themselves stuck to the ground.

[69] (*The Wedding Guests*):

Mˢ: Let her depart far from those she loves.

Tˢ: . . . the princess's in front of her father . . . With the bread, with the salt, with the thrice-holy image—

Bˢ: . . . and bless her all the same . . .

[70] (*Everybody*) and & [71]:

Tˢ: Saint Cosmas, Saint Cosmas, come with us, Saints Cosmas and Damian, come with us!

Sˢ: In the lower chamber, the beautiful one, the well-sprinkled one, two turtle-doves have alighted—

A.: Saint Cosmas blacksmith, choose your best nails, forge this marriage for us; Cosmas, forge it for us, forge it strong for us, forge it hard for us, so that the marriage lasts—

B.: Saints Cosmas and Damian have heard us; they have descended into the courtyard, they have come back with the nails.

[72] Tˢ: For the rest of our life.

S.A.T.B.: And until our grandchildren.

[73] Sˢ: In the lower chamber, the beautiful one, the well-sprinkled one—

S.A.: Two turtle-doves have alighted.

Tˢ: And there! we sing, we dance, we drink—

Sˢ: We bang the drum, we strike it with all our might.

[74] T.: Forge the marriage for us as you know how to do . . . from their youth to their old age.

B.: Saints Cosmas and Damian have heard us; they descended into the courtyard and then came back.

A.: Protect, unite the bride and groom from their youth to their old age.

Sˢ, Mˢ, Tˢ, Bˢ: And until their grandchildren.

[75] T.: And You, who gave Your Son—

Sˢ, Mˢ, S.A.: You, through whom Jesus Christ came into the world—

[76] T.: Come to the wedding and bless it—

Sˢ, Mˢ, S.A.: Keep the bride and groom united—

[77] Sˢ, Mˢ, Tˢ, Bˢ, S.A.T.B.: And all the Apostles as well, and all the saints in Paradise—

[78] & [79] Sˢ: And, just as around the trunk up to the tip the hop vine does, so may the bride and groom entwine around each other!

T.: And, just as around the trunk up to the tip . . . may the bride and groom, the bride and groom entwine around each other!

Mˢ, S.A.: The hop vine does, so may the bride and groom entwine around each other!

Tˢ: To the tip . . . may the bride and groom, the bride and groom entwine around each other!

Bˢ, B.: May the bride and groom, the bride and groom entwine around each other!

[80] (*The departure of the bride—everybody leaves the stage accompanying her.*)

[81] (*The stage remains empty.*)

[*In* [80] *&* [81] *the singers prolong the "oo" sound of their final syllable in* [79]. *Both the Russian and the French texts have this sound.*]

[82] (*The mothers of the groom and bride enter from different sides of the stage.*)

Sˢ: Dear child to whom I gave birth, dear child—

[83] & [84] Mˢ: You whom I have nursed and fed, you who were born of me, beloved child, beloved child, come back here; you have gone away, leaving the key hanging on the peg—

Sˢ: Dear child, don't make me wait; come back, child of my womb; come back quickly, come back—

[85] & [86] Sˢ: At the end of its silver ribbon; child to whom I gave birth . . .

Mˢ: Child to whom I gave birth . . .

(*The mothers exit. The stage remains empty.*)

PART TWO
Scene Four: The Wedding Feast

[87] S.A.T.B.: There are two flowers on the stem, one red and one white. The red one and the white one were on the stem—

Sˢ, Mˢ: Ay, luli, luli, luli! Lushenki, ay luli!

[*meaningless syllables; like "tra-la-la"*]

S.A.T.B.: Ay luli!

[88] Tˢ: A red one is there, is there!

T.B.: A red one!

Sˢ, Mˢ, S.A.: Ay luli!

Tˢ: A white one is there, is there!

Bˢ, T.B.: Is there!

Sˢ, Mˢ, S.A.: Ay, lushenki, luli!

Tˢ, Bˢ, T.B.: Ay, luli!

[89] Sˢ, Mˢ, Tˢ, S.A.T.: And see, the red one spoke to the white one; the white one was right beside it on the stem—

Bˢ, B.: Who is it that's coming? Curly Fyodor—

Sˢ, Mˢ, Tˢ, S.A.T.: And Sir Khvetis is the flower on the stem, [90] and Khvetis is the red one and Nastasia is the white one.

B.: Fyodor found the ring, [90] made of gold and adorned with a big ruby.

Bˢ: Who is it coming along so merrily?

Sˢ, Mˢ, S.: It's Mister Palagei.

Bˢ: What has happened to him?

Sˢ, Mˢ, S.: To Mister Palagei?

[91] Bˢ: He's lost the gilded ring, the ring adorned with a big ruby.

[92] S.A.T.: Hey, nonny-nonny, poor, poor Palagei, poor Palagei, he's no longer jolly, he's no longer jolly, poor Palagei.

B.: He's lost the ring that was gilded and adorned with a big ruby.

[93] Sˢ, Mˢ, Tˢ, Bˢ: Who has arrived, arrived? . . . The goose has arrived, arrived—

S.: The red one on the stem has leaned over toward the white one, the white one has leaned over to the red one on the branch, yu yu yu yu yu yu yu—

B.: Yu yu yu yu yu yu. Arrived? Yu yu yu yu yu yu. Arrived. Yu yu yu yu yu yu yu yu—

T.: Yu yu yu yu yu yu yu yu yu yu yu yu yu yu yu yu yu yu yu yu yu yu yu yu yu yu yu yu yu yu yu yu yu yu—

A.: Arrived? . . . Arrived. . . . Yu yu yu yu yu yu yu—

[94] Sˢ, Mˢ, Tˢ, Bˢ,. S.A.T.B.: Ho lai!

Tˢ: The goose has arrived—

Sˢ, Mˢ, Bˢ, S.A.T.B.: Ho!

Tˢ: It came in through the door, it came in.

[95] Sˢ, Mˢ, Bˢ, S.A.T.B.: Ho! Ho!

Sˢ, Mˢ: It flapped its wings so hard—

Tˢ: That they broke—

Sˢ, Mˢ: Ho, la li la li lai!

Tˢ: It made the walls shake—

[96] Tˢ, Bˢ, T. B.: Ho lai!

Sˢ, Mˢ, S.A.: Ho lai!

Tˢ: And woke us up—

Tˢ, Bˢ, T.B.: Ho lai!

Sˢ, Mˢ, S.A.: Ho lai! Ho la li lai!

Bˢ (*The Groom's Father*): There is the woman—

B.: The woman—

Tˢ: Whom God himself gave you.

[97] T.B. (*The Men*): You, woman, sow the flax.

Sˢ, Mˢ, S.A. (*The Women*): What did they say to you, tell me, bride?

T.B. (*The Men*): She'll have to keep your linens good and clean—

Tˢ: The shirts, the shorts!

Sˢ, Mˢ, S.A. (*The Women*): And tell me, sweetie, what did they say to you?

[98] (*The bride's mother brings her over to her son-in-law.*)

Mˢ: My beloved son-in-law, I entrust my beloved child to your care.

(*The Best Man, the Groom's Mother, The Male Matchmaker and The Female Matchmaker, in turn*):

Tˢ: You, sow the flax—

Mˢ: You, ask her for your shirts—

Bˢ, Mˢ: Be in the cellar and the attic—

[99] Sˢ, Tˢ: From morning to night, be up, be up and on your feet.

M^s: Supervise the help.

S.A.T.: Be up and on your feet.

B^s: Chop the wood—

B.: The wood—

S.: After that—

[100] S.A.T.B.: Smack—

T^s: Love her—

B.: Like your soul—

B^s, T^s: Love her like your soul—

T^s, B^s, T.B.: Shake her like a plum tree.

[101] S.A.: Our gentlefolk came, they laughed, they drank—

T.B.: They went around all the tables—

S.A.: They laughed, they drank, our gentlefolk came, they drank a toast with Marya—

[102] T.B.: Drank a toast with Marya:—

B^s: Drink, pretty Marya, eat and fill yourself up.

S^s: I won't eat or [103] drink, I won't listen to you.

B^s: And what if it were your good friend?

S^s: I would've eaten and drunk, I'd have had a good laugh, too.

[104] S.A.: Hey, gray skirt over there, you prowling around—

T^s, B^s, B.: The one who's not from here—

S.A.: Where are you from, goose, where are you from, gray one?

[105] B.: The one who's not from here, where are you from, beauty, and what have you seen?

S.A.: You who come from afar, where are you from?

T.: Where are you from, beauty, and what have you seen?

[106] S^s: I was far away on the sea, I was far away on the enormous sea—

S.A.: Luli, luli, far away on the enormous sea—

[107] S^s: The white maiden was bathing there, washing her white dress in it—

S.A.: Luli! Washing her Sunday dress.

[108] M^s: Had he seen the maiden?

M^s, B^s: Had the white swan seen his mate?

T^s: How could I not have been there, how, how would I have acted?

S.A.: How, how could I not have seen her when she was there?

[109] B^s: Where, where is the swan and also his mate, where? Wherever he tarries, she tarries beneath his wing. Where, where is Khvetis and also the woman he loves? Wherever she is lying, he is lying alongside her.

S^s: . . . Over there two white swans were swimming, over there on the sea they were swimming—

A.: . . . Oh, luli, oh, luli! Two swans far from here.

S.: . . . Two swans far from here.

[110] (A Male Guest on the Bride's Side):

T^s: And you, why do you think so much of yourself?

B^s: And you over there—

S^s (The Bride): Down to my waist I am hung with gold, my pearled flounces trail along the ground.

[111] B^s (The Male Matchmaker): Drunkard, dirty swine, father of Nastasia . . .

T^s (A Male Guest): Hey, over there, get a move on, boys, bring us the bride, the groom is bored all alone!

B.: For a glass of wine you sold your daughter . . .

B^s: . . . and today it's your daughter you're drinking!

[112] T^s (The same Male Guest): Hey! you where-did-you-come-froms and you worth-nothings, you girls who can be had for two sous, and you backbiters, [113] and you women who look like Germans, and you with runny noses and unwiped behinds, bare-assed and shoeless—all of you come here!

[114] (A male guest [on the groom's side] chooses a man and woman from among the guests and sends them to warm the bed for the married pair.)

S.A. (The Girls): He said:

S^s, M^s, T^s: "I'm going."

S.A.: She said:

S^s, M^s, T^s: "Take me along."

S.A.: He said:

S^s, M^s, T^s: "The bed is narrow."

S.A.: She said:

S^s, M^s, T^s: "We'll manage."

S.A.: He said:

S^s, M^s, T^s: "You know, the sheets are cold."

S.A.: She said:

S^s, M^s, T^s: "We'll warm them up."

[115] S.: It's for you, Khvetis, that we sing the song of the pair together. For the red flower and the white, which are together on the branch.

[116] S^s, M^s, S.A.: Do you hear, do you hear, Khvetis? Do you hear, Pamfilevich?

S.A.: We sing you the song of the girl and boy.

[117] (The Male Matchmaker and the Guests):

B^s: What's wrong with you there, . . .

B^s, B.: . . . snoring like that?

B^s: Hey, get up, Savelyushka, [118] come, get a move on!

B^s, B.: There are things . . .

B^s: . . . to do over there!

[119] (The Guests):

S.A.: Where people have fun, they drink, and where they drink, everything goes.

T^s, T.: Our gentlefolk have come, they said it's well known:

T^s, B^s, T.B.: We know how to do things; . . .

[120] B^s: With us, weddings are celebrated in the finest way, . . .

B^s, B.: At our place, we drink nine kinds of wine, . . .

T^s, B^s, T.B.: And the tenth kind is unique in the world.

[121] S^s, M^s, A.: Our Nastasia is going away for good to a strange country.

S^s, M^s, S.A.: If she handles things right . . .

S^s, M^s, T^s, B^s, S.A.T.B.: . . . all will be well!

S^s, M^s, A: Let her be submissive, let her be resigned.

T^s, B^s, T.B.: All will be well!

S: All will go well for the girl.

[122] S^s: For a head that's resigned there's never a lack of pillows.

(The Guests, in turn):

xxii

S[s], T[s]: Give the poor man as well as the rich man a pretty smile . . .

[123] S[s], M[s], T[s]: And give your little husband a much prettier one.

B[s]: And all along the street . . .

B[s], B.: All along the boy goes . . .

S[s], M[s], S.A.: Goes into the green garden behind his Nastasia and looks at Nastasia, looks at her and thinks:

T[s]: In the street and all along goes the boy.

B[s]: In the street and all along . . . He has lovely trousers, lovely trousers.

T.: The boy goes . . . a derby hat.

B.: Lovely trousers.

[124] T[s]: My Nastasia walks with a light gait, her coat is of cloth of gold with a beaver collar.

T[s], T. (*The Male Guests*): Ah! her pretty black eyebrows!

[125] T[s] (*A Male Guest*): All right, fellow, now empty your glass!

S.A.T. (*The other Male Guests and the Women*): That's clear, empty your glass!

T.: And then, don't forget the presents!

S.A.T.: Don't forget the presents!

T[s]: The young couple need loads of things. First of all they want to have a beautiful house.

B[s]: A really good one.

T[s]: And then they'll want to enlarge it . . . [126] and then they'll beautify it and then they'll boast: "We know how to live well, don't we, friends?"

(*The Guests*):

B[s]: The wine has an odd taste, it sticks in your throat!

T.B.: It sticks in your throat!

S[s], M[s], T[s], S.A.: You must add sugar to it!

(*The bride and groom kiss.*)

B[s]: You must drink, and a lot—

S[s], M[s], S.A.: The wine has an odd taste . . .

T[s]: It sticks, it sticks in your throat!

S[s], M[s], S.A.T.: It sticks in your throat!

[127] B[s]: That woman, that woman is worth around ten sous, ten sous, ten sous; that's not much.

B[s], B.: If, if someone got a child on her . . .

[128] B[s]: . . . she'd be worth twice, . . .

B[s], B.: . . . twice as much.

T.: Then as for me . . .

(*The Male Guests*):

T[s], B[s], part of B.: In the house there is singing.

T.: . . . me, me, I don't give a damn, but . . .

Rest of B.: I don't give a damn.

S.A. (*The Women*): And in front of the door there is lamenting:

T., B.: . . . we won't be . . .

B.: . . . won't be at the end.

[129] S[s], M[s], B[s], S.A.T.: "Where are you, ugly woman? Where are you, spiteful woman?"

B.: If it's this gentleman who's laying out, laying out the money, it, it'll cost him around a hundred francs.

T[s] (*A Male Guest*): Hey, over there, haven't you seen that the girl can't take any more?

S[s], M[s]: Look at her sulking.

S.A.: She jogs him with her elbow.

T[s]: She's turned toward him.

B[s] (*The Male Matchmaker, to the couple who are warming the bed*): So that she can sulk better, she should be put to bed.

[130] (*Those who were warming the bed exit. Khvetis and Nastasia are led up to the bed and made to lie down, then they are left alone and the door is shut. The two fathers and the two mothers sit down on a bench in front of the door; all the rest are opposite them.*)

S[s], M[s], S.T.: The beautiful well-made bed, the beautiful square bed!

A.B.: On the bed there is the feather mattress . . .

S[s], M[s], S.T.: And right beside it there is the pillow.

A.: There is the pillow, and right beside it the pillow.

T[s]: And the pillow is located right beside it.

B.: Right beside it.

[131] S[s]: And under the pillow the well-smoothed sheets.

S.A.T.: And right beside it the well-smoothed sheets.

T[s]: And under the sheets, there is someone hidden.

B[s]: It's Khvetis, it's curly-headed Khvetis, . . .

B.: Curly-headed Khvetis, . . .

M[s], A.: And the sparrow found its nest, . . .

M[s], A.: . . . he holds his mate tight.

T[s], B[s]: . . . Khvetis Pamfilevich.

[132] S[s], M[s], S.A.: He holds her tight, he has put her in his bed.

T[ss], B[s], T.B.: He has taken his Nastasiushka in his arms, . . .

T[s], B[s]: . . . has taken her in his arms, has pressed her to his heart.

S[s], M[s], S.A.T.: He has pressed her, pressed her to his . . .

S[s], M[s], T[s], B[s], S.A.T.B.: . . . heart:

[133] B[s]: "Well, my darling, my sweetheart, flower of my days, honey of my nights, honey of my nights, flower of my life, I shall live with you [134] the way people are supposed to live, so that the others envy us, so that we make them envious."

(*The curtain is slowly lowered during all of the following music.*)

LES NOCES

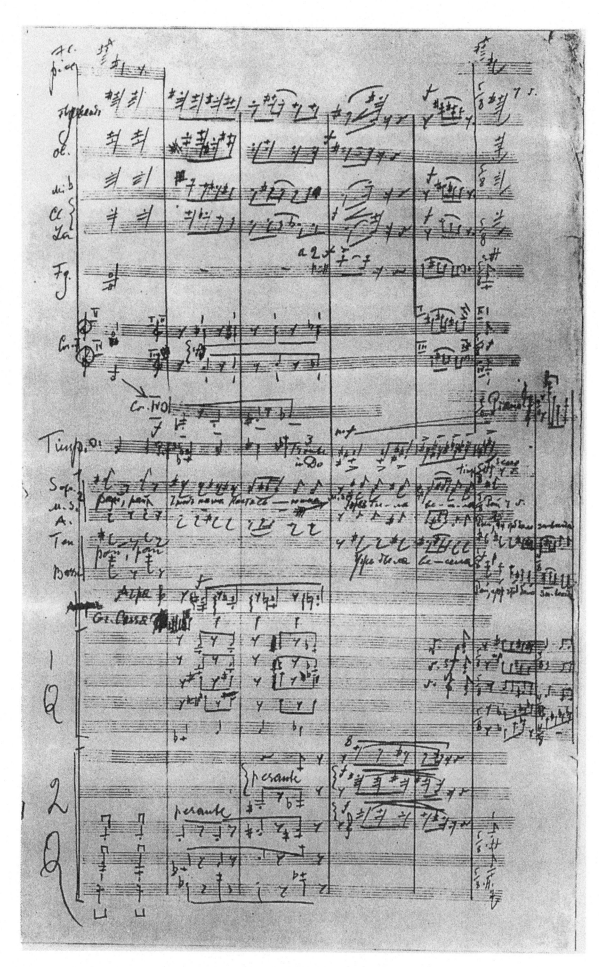

MS. sketch of *Les Noces*, section 17,
showing the first projected scheme of orchestration.

(*From the collection of Lord Berners*)

A Serge de Diaghilew

СВАДЕБКА	LES NOCES
ЧАСТЬ ПЕРВАЯ	PREMIÈRE PARTIE
КАРТИНА ПЕРВАЯ	PREMIER TABLEAU
„КОСА"	„LA TRESSE"

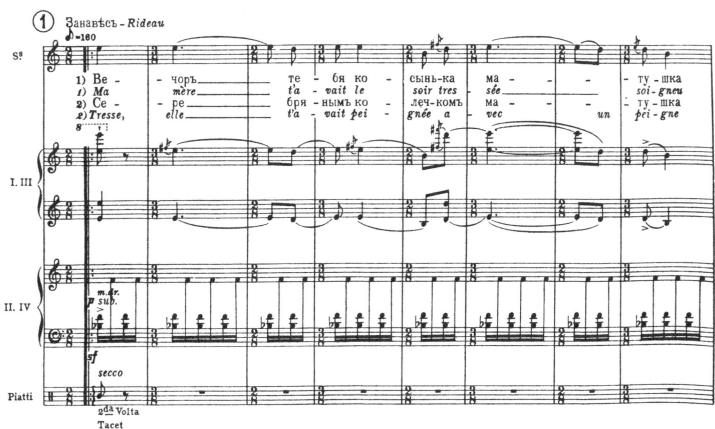

attaca subita

КАРТИНА ВТОРАЯ
У ЖЕНИХА

DEUXIÈME TABLEAU
CHEZ LE MARIÉ

24

* "*fr*⁓" signifie *frôler la membrane avec le pouce*

КАРТИНА ТРЕТЬЯ
ПРОВОДЫ НЕВѢСТЫ

TROISIÈME TABLEAU
LE DÉPART DE LA MARIÉE

64

66

73

(Женихов дружка выбирает изъ поѣзжанъ одного мужа и жену и ведетъ ихъ обоспать для молодыхъ постель.)
(Un ami de noces choisit parmi les invités un homme et sa femme et les envoie chauffer le lit pour les mariés.)

120

129
(Одинъ изъ дружекъ)
(Un des amis de noces)
Sᵍ
„Ахъ тёш-ша мо-я, тёш-ша лас-ко-ва-я!"
„Où est tu vi-lai-ne? où est tu mé-chan-te?"
M.Sᵍ
Tᵍ
ff
Ай, вы дружки
(pour le français)
Tᵍ
ff
Eh, là
Bᵍ
„Ахъ тёш-ша мо-я, тёш-ша лас-ко-ва-я!"
„Où est tu vi-lai-ne? où est tu mé-chan-te?"
S.
-ротъ у-би-ва-ет-ся:
porte on se la-men-te:
„Ахъ тёш-ша мо-я, тёш-ша лас-ко-ва-я!"
„Où est tu vi-lai-ne? où est tu mé-chan-te?"
A.
T.
„Ахъ тёш-ша мо-я, тёш-ша лас-ко-ва-я!"
„Où est tu vi-lai-ne? où est tu mé-chan-te?"
B.
хоть бы пять
s(e)ra pas au bout
А ког-да
Si c'est monsieur
I
8ª bassa
II
8ª bassa
III
8ª bassa
IV
8ª bassa
C.cl.
Tmb.
s.t.
come sopra
come sopra
Gr.C.

Настасью ведутъ къ постели, укладываютъ ихъ, запираютъ дверь и оставляютъ однихъ. Родители жен. и нев. усаживаются на скамьѣ передъ дверью. Всѣ обращены къ нимъ лицомъ.
et on ferme la porte. Les deux pères et les deux mères s'installent devant la porte sur un banc, tout le monde leur faisant face.

Занавѣсъ опускается медленно впродолженіе всей послѣдующей музыки
Le rideau se baisse lentement durant toute la musique suivante.

Dover Opera, Choral and Lieder Scores

Bach, Johann Sebastian, EASTER ORATORIO IN FULL SCORE. Reproduces the authoritative Bach-Gesellschaft edition, in which the vocal parts of the third version of the oratorio were collated with the score of the first revision in an attempt to discover Bach's final intentions. Instrumentation. New English translation of text. 80pp. 9 x 12. 0-486-41890-1

Bach, Johann Sebastian, ELEVEN GREAT CANTATAS. Full vocal-instrumental score from Bach-Gesellschaft edition. *Christ lag in Todesbanden, Ich hatte viel Bekümmerniss, Jauchhzet Gott in allen Landen,* eight others. Study score. 350pp. 9 x 12. 0-486-23268-9

Bach, Johann Sebastian, MASS IN B MINOR IN FULL SCORE. The crowning glory of Bach's lifework in the field of sacred music and a universal statement of Christian faith, reprinted from the authoritative Bach-Gesellschaft edition. Translation of texts. 320pp. 9 x 12. 0-486-25992-7

Bach, Johann Sebastian, SEVEN GREAT SACRED CANTATAS IN FULL SCORE. Seven favorite sacred cantatas. Printed from a clear, modern engraving and sturdily bound; new literal line-for-line translations. Reliable Bach-Gesellschaft edition. Complete German texts. 256pp. 9 x 12. 0-486-24950-6

Bach, Johann Sebastian, SIX GREAT SECULAR CANTATAS IN FULL SCORE. Bach's nearest approach to comic opera. *Hunting Cantata, Wedding Cantata, Aeolus Appeased, Phoebus and Pan, Coffee Cantata,* and *Peasant Cantata.* 286pp. 9 x 12. 0-486-23934-9

Beethoven, Ludwig van, FIDELIO IN FULL SCORE. Beethoven's only opera, complete in one affordable volume, including all spoken German dialogue. Republication of C. F. Peters, Leipzig edition. 272pp. 9 x 12. 0-486-24740-6

Bizet, Georges, CARMEN IN FULL SCORE. Complete, authoritative score of perhaps the world's most popular opera, in the version most commonly performed today, with recitatives by Ernest Guiraud. 574pp. 9 x 12. 0-486-25820-3

Brahms, Johannes, COMPLETE SONGS FOR SOLO VOICE AND PIANO (two volumes). A total of 113 songs in complete score by greatest lieder writer since Schubert. Series I contains 15-song cycle *Die Schone Magelone*; Series II includes famous "Lullaby." Total of 448pp. 9⅜ x 12¼. Series I: 0-486-23820-2; Series II: 0-486-23821-0

Brahms, Johannes, COMPLETE SONGS FOR SOLO VOICE AND PIANO: Series III. 64 songs, published from 1877 to 1886, include such favorites as "Geheimnis," "Alte Liebe," and "Vergebliches Standchen." 224pp. 9 x 12. 0-486-23822-9

Brahms, Johannes, COMPLETE SONGS FOR SOLO VOICE AND PIANO: Series IV. 120 songs that complete the Brahms song oeuvre, with sensitive arrangements of 91 folk and traditional songs. 240pp. 9 x 12. 0-486-23823-7

Brahms, Johannes, GERMAN REQUIEM IN FULL SCORE. Definitive Breitkopf & Härtel edition of Brahms's greatest vocal work, fully scored for solo voices, mixed chorus and orchestra. 208pp. 9⅜ x 12¼. 0-486-25486-0

Debussy, Claude, PELLÉAS ET MÉLISANDE IN FULL SCORE. Reprinted from the E. Fromont (1904) edition, this volume faithfully reproduces the full orchestral-vocal score of Debussy's sole and enduring opera masterpiece. 416pp. 9 x 12. (Available in U.S. only) 0-486-24825-9

Debussy, Claude, SONGS, 1880–1904. Rich selection of 36 songs set to texts by Verlaine, Baudelaire, Pierre Louÿs, Charles d'Orleans, others. 175pp. 9 x 12. 0-486-24131-9

Fauré, Gabriel, SIXTY SONGS. "Clair de lune," "Apres un reve," "Chanson du pecheur," "Automne," and other great songs set for medium voice. Reprinted from French editions. 288pp. 8⅜ x 11. (Not available in France or Germany) 0-486-26534-X

Gilbert, W. S. and Sullivan, Sir Arthur, THE AUTHENTIC GILBERT & SULLIVAN SONGBOOK, 92 songs, uncut, original keys, in piano renderings approved by Sullivan. 399pp. 9 x 12. 0-486-23482-7

Gilbert, W. S. and Sullivan, Sir Arthur, HMS PINAFORE IN FULL SCORE. New edition by Carl Simpson and Ephraim Hammett Jones. Some of Gilbert's most clever flashes of wit and a number of Sullivan's most charming melodies in a handsome, authoritative new edition based on original manuscripts and early sources. 256pp. 9 x 12. 0-486-42201-1

Gilbert, W. S. and Sullivan, Sir Arthur (Carl Simpson and Ephraim Hammett Jones, eds.), THE PIRATES OF PENZANCE IN FULL SCORE. New performing edition corrects numerous errors, offers performers the choice of two versions of the Act II finale, and gives the first accurate full score of the "Climbing over Rocky Mountain" section. 288pp. 9 x 12. 0-486-41891-X

Grieg, Edvard, FIFTY SONGS FOR HIGH VOICE. Outstanding compilation includes many of his most popular melodies, such as "Solvejg's Song," "From Monte Pincio," and "Dreams." Introduction. Notes. 176pp. 9 x 12. 0-486-44130-X

Hale, Philip (ed.), FRENCH ART SONGS OF THE NINETEENTH CENTURY: 39 Works from Berlioz to Debussy. 39 songs from romantic period by 18 composers: Berlioz, Chausson, Debussy (six songs), Gounod, Massenet, Thomas, etc. French text, English singing translation for high voice. 182pp. 9 x 12. (Not available in France or Germany) 0-486-23680-3

Handel, George Frideric, GIULIO CESARE IN FULL SCORE. Great Baroque masterpiece reproduced directly from authoritative Deutsche Handelgesellschaft edition. Gorgeous melodies, inspired orchestration. Complete and unabridged. 160pp. 9⅜ x 12¼. 0-486-25056-3

Handel, George Frideric, MESSIAH IN FULL SCORE. An authoritative full-score edition of the oratorio that is the best-known, most-beloved, most-performed large-scale musical work in the English-speaking world. 240pp. 9 x 12. 0-486-26067-4

Monteverdi, Claudio, MADRIGALS: BOOK IV & V. 39 finest madrigals with new line-for-line literal English translations of the poems facing the Italian text. 256pp. 8⅛ x 11. (Available in U.S. only) 0-486-25102-0

Mozart, Wolfgang Amadeus, THE ABDUCTION FROM THE SERAGLIO IN FULL SCORE. Mozart's early comic masterpiece, exactingly reproduced from the authoritative Breitkopf & Härtel edition. 320pp. 9 x 12. 0-486-26004-6

Mozart, Wolfgang Amadeus, COSI FAN TUTTE IN FULL SCORE. Scholarly edition of one of Mozart's greatest operas. Da Ponte libretto. Commentary. Preface. Translated Front Matter. 448pp. 9⅜ x 12¼. (Available in U.S. only) 0-486-24528-4

Mozart, Wolfgang Amadeus, DON GIOVANNI: COMPLETE ORCHESTRAL SCORE. Full score that contains everything from the original version, along with later arias, recitatives, and duets added to original score for Vienna performance. Peters edition. Study score. 468pp. 9⅜ x 12¼. (Available in U.S. only) 0-486-23026-0

Mozart, Wolfgang Amadeus, THE MAGIC FLUTE (DIE ZAUBERFLÖTE) IN FULL SCORE. Authoritative C. F. Peters edition of Mozart's brilliant last opera still widely popular. Includes all the spoken dialogue. 226pp. 9 x 12. 0-486-24783-X

Mozart, Wolfgang Amadeus, THE MARRIAGE OF FIGARO: COMPLETE SCORE. Finest comic opera ever written. Full score, beautifully engraved, includes passages often cut in other editions. Peters edition. Study score. 448pp. 9⅜ x 12¼. (Available in U.S. only) 0-486-23751-6

*Available from your music dealer or write for **free** Music Catalog to*
Dover Publications, Inc., Dept. MUBI, 31 East 2nd Street, Mineola, NY 11501
*Visit us online at **www.doverpublications.com***

Dover Opera, Choral and Lieder Scores

Mozart, Wolfgang Amadeus, REQUIEM IN FULL SCORE. Masterpiece of vocal composition, among the most recorded and performed works in the repertoire. Authoritative edition published by Breitkopf & Härtel, Wiesbaden. 203pp. 8⅜ x 11¼. 0-486-25311-2

Offenbach, Jacques, OFFENBACH'S SONGS FROM THE GREAT OPERETTAS. Piano, vocal (French text) for 38 most popular songs: *Orphée, Belle Hélène, Vie Parisienne, Duchesse de Gérolstein,* others. 21 illustrations. 195pp. 9 x 12. 0-486-23341-3

Prokokiev, Sergei, THE LOVE FOR THREE ORANGES VOCAL SCORE. Surrealistic fairy tale satirizes traditional operatic forms with a daring and skillful combination of humor, sorrow, fantasy, and grotesquery. Russian and French texts. iv+252pp. 7½ x 10¾. (Available in the U.S. only.) 0-486-44169-5

Puccini, Giacomo, LA BOHÈME IN FULL SCORE. Authoritative Italian edition of one of the world's most beloved operas. English translations of list of characters and instruments. 416pp. 8⅜ x 11¼. (Not available in United Kingdom, France, Germany or Italy) 0-486-25477-1

Rachmaninoff, Serge, THE BELLS IN FULL SCORE. Written for large orchestra, solo vocalists, and chorus, loosely based on Poe's brilliant poem with added material from the Russian translation that permits Rachmaninoff to develop the themes in a more intense, dark idiom. x+118pp. 9⅜ x 12¼. 0-486-44149-0

Rossini, Gioacchino, THE BARBER OF SEVILLE IN FULL SCORE. One of the greatest comic operas ever written, reproduced here directly from the authoritative score published by Ricordi. 464pp. 8⅜ x 11¼. 0-486-26019-4

Schubert, Franz, COMPLETE SONG CYCLES. Complete piano, vocal music of *Die Schöne Müllerin, Die Winterreise, Schwanengesang.* Also Drinker English singing translations. Breitkopf & Härtel edition. 217pp. 9⅜ x 12¼. 0-486-22649-2

Schubert, Franz, SCHUBERT'S SONGS TO TEXTS BY GOETHE. Only one-volume edition of Schubert's Goethe songs from authoritative Breitkopf & Härtel edition, plus all revised versions. New prose translation of poems. 84 songs. 256pp. 9⅜ x 12¼. 0-486-23752-4

Schubert, Franz, 59 FAVORITE SONGS. "Der Wanderer," "Ave Maria," "Hark, Hark, the Lark," and 56 other masterpieces of lieder reproduced from the Breitkopf & Härtel edition. 256pp. 9⅜ x 12¼. 0-486-24849-6

Schumann, Robert, SELECTED SONGS FOR SOLO VOICE AND PIANO. Over 100 of Schumann's greatest lieder, set to poems by Heine, Goethe, Byron, others. Breitkopf & Härtel edition. 248pp. 9⅜ x 12¼. 0-486-24202-1

Strauss, Richard, DER ROSENKAVALIER IN FULL SCORE. First inexpensive edition of great operatic masterpiece, reprinted complete and unabridged from rare, limited Fürstner edition (1910) approved by Strauss. 528pp. 9⅜ x 12¼. (Available in U.S. only) 0-486-25498-4

Strauss, Richard, DER ROSENKAVALIER: VOCAL SCORE. Inexpensive edition reprinted directly from original Fürstner (1911) edition of vocal score. Verbal text, vocal line and piano "reduction." 448pp. 8⅜ x 11¼. (Not available in Europe or the United Kingdom) 0-486-25501-8

Strauss, Richard, SALOME IN FULL SCORE. Atmospheric color predominates in composer's first great operatic success. Definitive Fürstner score, now extremely rare. 352pp. 9⅜ x 12¼. (Available in U.S. only) 0-486-24208-0

Stravinsky, Igor, SONGS 1906–1920. Brilliant interpretations of Russian folk songs collected for the first time in a single affordable volume. All scores are for voice and piano, with instrumental ensemble accompaniments to "Three Japanese Lyrics," "Pribaoutki," and "Berceuses du Chat" in full score as well as piano reduction. xiv+144pp. 9 x 12. 0-486-43821-X

Verdi, Giuseppe, AÏDA IN FULL SCORE. Verdi's glorious, most popular opera, reprinted from an authoritative edition published by G. Ricordi, Milan. 448pp. 9 x 12. 0-486-26172-7

Verdi, Giuseppe, FALSTAFF. Verdi's last great work, his first and only comedy. Complete unabridged score from original Ricordi edition. 480pp. 8⅜ x 11¼. 0-486-24017-7

Verdi, Giuseppe, OTELLO IN FULL SCORE. The penultimate Verdi opera, his tragic masterpiece. Complete unabridged score from authoritative Ricordi edition, with Front Matter translated. 576pp. 8¼ x 11. 0-486-25040-7

Verdi, Giuseppe, REQUIEM IN FULL SCORE. Immensely popular with choral groups and music lovers. Republication of edition published by C. F. Peters, Leipzig. Study score. 204pp. 9⅜ x 12¼. (Available in U.S. only) 0-486-23682-X

Wagner, Richard, DAS RHEINGOLD IN FULL SCORE. Complete score, clearly reproduced from B. Schott's authoritative edition. New translation of German Front Matter. 328pp. 9 x 12. 0-486-24925-5

Wagner, Richard, DIE MEISTERSINGER VON NÜRNBERG. Landmark in history of opera, in complete vocal and orchestral score of one of the greatest comic operas. C. F. Peters edition, Leipzig. Study score. 823pp. 8¼ x 11. 0-486-23276-X

Wagner, Richard, DIE WALKÜRE. Complete orchestral score of the most popular of the operas in the Ring Cycle. Reprint of the edition published in Leipzig by C. F. Peters, ca. 1910. Study score. 710pp. 8⅜ x 11¼. 0-486-23566-1

Wagner, Richard, THE FLYING DUTCHMAN IN FULL SCORE. Great early masterpiece reproduced directly from limited Weingartner edition (1896), incorporating Wagner's revisions. Text, stage directions in English, German, Italian. 432pp. 9⅜ x 12¼. 0-486-25629-4

Wagner, Richard, GÖTTERDÄMMERUNG. Full operatic score, first time available in U.S. Reprinted directly from rare 1877 first edition. 615pp. 9⅜ x 12¼. 0-486-24250-1

Wagner, Richard, PARSIFAL IN FULL SCORE. Composer's deeply personal treatment of the legend of the Holy Grail, renowned for splendid music, glowing orchestration. C. F. Peters edition. 592pp. 8¼ x 11. 0-486-25175-6

Wagner, Richard, SIEGFRIED IN FULL SCORE. *Siegfried,* third opera of Wagner's famous Ring Cycle, is reproduced from first edition (1876). 439pp. 9⅜ x 12¼. 0-486-24456-3

Wagner, Richard, TANNHAUSER IN FULL SCORE. Reproduces the original 1845 full orchestral and vocal score as slightly amended in 1847. Included is the ballet music for Act I written for the 1861 Paris production. 576pp. 8⅜ x 11¼. 0-486-24649-3

Wagner, Richard, TRISTAN UND ISOLDE. Full orchestral score with complete instrumentation. Study score. 655pp. 8⅛ x 11. 0-486-22915-7

von Weber, Carl Maria, DER FREISCHÜTZ. Full orchestral score to first Romantic opera, forerunner to Wagner and later developments. Still very popular. Study score, including full spoken text. 203pp. 9 x 12. 0-486-23449-5

Wolf, Hugo, THE COMPLETE MÖRIKE SONGS. Splendid settings to music of 53 German poems by Eduard Mörike, including "Der Tambour," "Elfenlied," and "Verborganheit." New prose translations. 208pp. 9⅜ x 12¼. 0-486-24380-X

Wolf, Hugo, SPANISH AND ITALIAN SONGBOOKS. Total of 90 songs by great 19th-century master of the genre. Reprint of authoritative C. F. Peters edition. New Translations of German texts. 256pp. 9⅜ x 12¼. 0-486-26156-5